MicroSculptures

Idols of the Stone Age to the Helix of Contemporary Genetics

Published by: The Ilias Lalaounis Jewelry Museum
12 *Kallisperi - Karyatidon St., Athens 117-42*

for the exhibition: *"Ilias Lalaounis: Micro-sculptures: Idols of the Stone Age to the Helix of Contemporary Genetics"*

at the ALEXANDER S. ONASSIS
PUBLIC BENEFIT FOUNDATION (USA)
ONASSIS CULTURAL CENTER
Olympic Tower
645 Fifth Avenue
New York, N.Y. 10022-5910

ISBN: 960-7417-12-7

Ilias LALAoUNIS

MicroSculptures

Idols of the Stone Age to the Helix of Contemporary Genetics

IOANNA LALAOUNIS TSOUKOPOULOU

1 November 2001 - 10 February 2002
ONASSIS CULTURAL CENTER - OLYMPIC TOWER
New York

ALEXANDER S. ONASSIS PUBLIC BENEFIT FOUNDATION
ILIAS LALAOUNIS JEWELRY MUSEUM

THE EXHIBITION

GENERAL ORGANIZATION
Ioanna Lalaounis Tsoukopoulou

ADMINISTRATION MANAGEMENT
Marina Azaria

CURATORIAL CO-ORDINATION
Ioannis Kotoulas

PRESS OFFICE
Angie Nomikou

SPECIAL DECORATIONS ADVISOR
Katerini Lalaounis

RESTORATION CO-ORDINATION
Maria Lalaounis

SET UP MANAGEMENT
Nikitas Tsakiris

DECORATORS
Carlos Finsterbusch
Georgios Kotsaris

VIDEO PRODUCTION
Constantinos Tseklenis

EDUCATIONAL MATERIAL
Maria Gavrilou
Ioannis Kotoulas
Grigoris Grigorakakis

INSURANCE
Liana Lambroukou
with "Alpha Insurance"

TRANSPORT OF WORKS
Orphée Beinoglou, SA

SUPPORT MATERIAL, PRINTING
"Dot Imaging" Dimitris Kokkoris

GRAPHIC DESIGNERS
Spiros Theodorou
Daphne Marketou

THE CATALOGUE

Ioanna Lalaounis Tsoukopoulou

EDITING, PROOF READING
Alexandra Doumas

RESEARCH
Ioannis Kotoulas
Grigoris Grigorakakis
Haralambos Raptis

PHOTOGRAPHS
Ch. Iossifides & G. Moutevelis
Nikos Baxevanoglou
Nikos Kokkolias

PHOTOGRAPHIC ARCHIVES
Ilias Lalaounis Jewelry Museum

ARTISTIC DESIGN
Kristy Kasastoyianni
Fotini Sakellari

PRODUCTION COORDINATOR
Efi Vouveli

PUBLICATION PRODUCTION
Adam Editions
Pergamos Ekdotiki-Ektypotiki S.A.I.C.

Front Cover: Rock-crystal sealstone representing the Ocean, from the Shield of Achilles Collection (1978)

CONTENTS

GOLD AND PRECIOUS STONES have always fascinated man, exciting the eye and the mind alike, even in their native state.

For their sake, wars have been waged and crimes committed, men have vowed everlasting love and sworn eternal hatred. The powerful have used them to enhance their status and impose their might upon enemy and ally. Saint and sinner admire them alike.

In the hands of the artist they become truly irresistible, especially when the artist is a master goldsmith and a gifted jeweler of the stature of Ilias Lalaounis.

We at the Onassis Foundation (both parent and affiliated) are pleased to host, at the Onassis Cultural Center in New York, the *objets d' art,* that are a major part of the micro-sculptures from the permanent collections of the Ilias Lalaounis Jewelry Museum, created by a man of art, culture and vision. We wish to share with others the refined pleasure given by beauty in its purest, but by no means, simplest form.

I have the honour and the pleasure of inviting you to share this exhibition with us, so that you may enjoy the splendid art of Ilias Lalaounis.

STELIO A. PAPADIMITRIOU
PRESIDENT

INTRODUCTION

THE JEWELRY AND MICRO SCULPTURES produced by Ilias Lalaounis are renowned for their inspiration, craftsmanship and elegance. This catalogue focuses on selected *objets d'art* designed and presented between 1970-2000, a period in which Lalaounis produced thousands of original designs, many of which were given concrete form as unique pieces, as special commissions and for his international clientele.

Ilias Lalaounis, born in 1920 in the heart of Athens, is today acclaimed worldwide as an artist and jeweler. He started work in the family business in 1940, and founded his own company in 1968, today known as Greek Gold - Ilias Lalaounis S. A. At first branches were opened on several Greek islands, quickly followed by stores in major European cities, New York, Tokyo and Hong Kong. Lalaounis has received many honors for his art, the most notable being from the *Institut de France, Académie des Beaux Arts,* in 1990, when he became the only jeweler ever elected as a member.

The 1940s, when Lalaounis began his career, were troubled times for Greece, both politically and economically. He looked for new ways of promoting the business, at first making necklace and bracelet chains and later focusing on the art of gem-setting, on jewels. In the mid-1950s he decided to break away from established jewelry and turned to the revival of designs and techniques from Antiquity, making ornaments and objects in silver, 18ct and 22ct gold. This ingenious idea proved successful and was, without doubt, a turning point in his life and work. Ancient artifacts sparked off his imagination and inspired jewelry designs for today's woman as well as hundreds of decorative and functional *objets d'art* for the modern home and office.

Lalaounis's knowledge and grasp of the art and history of early civilizations led him to create a number of 'archaeological collections', based on various cultures of Europe, Asia and America. In the 1970s he proved his inexhaustible ability to search for new ideas by designing spectacular pieces based on the achievements of modern technology, astronomy, nature and medicine, to mention but a few.

For this exhibition "*Micro sculptures: Idols from the Stone Age to the Helix of Contemporary Genetics*", 240 micro-sculptures have been chosen from the permanent collections of the Ilias Lalaounis Jewelry Museum (ILJM) in Athens. Founded in 1993, the ILJM not only provides a home for Lalaounis's best creations since 1940 but also aims at becoming a center for jewelry studies. Archives of drawings, plaster casts, audio-visual material, photographs and over 3000 items (jewelry and *objets d' art*) from Lalaounis's vast *oeuvre* complement the pieces exhibited in the Museum's fifty collections.

The six collections chosen here draw fully on all aspects of Lalaounis's research in the fascinating fields of archaeology, the natural environment and modern technology. Unpublished designs and works not previously shown to the public are displayed along with objects that have already traveled to exhibitions in France, Tokyo, the USA, Switzerland, the United Kingdom, Iran, Turkey and Russia.

This exhibition in the Onassis Cultural Center, in the Olympic Tower in New York, is the first presentation of Lalaounis's work devoted exclusively to micro-sculptures. Although much has been omitted, it is a representative selection of the other side of the renowned jeweler's activity. His passion for the *objet d'art* and micro-sculpture is illustrated by this assemblage of original works in semi-precious stones, 18ct gold, silver, gold-plated silver and bronze. The style of these objects, with their plasticity of form and a three-dimensional quality, reflects the designs used in his jewelry, since similar techniques and materials are used. Lalaounis's intuitive interest in archaeology and classical literature led him to recreate ancient symbols in modern works of art. He recreated Paleolithic cave paintings on engraved semiprecious stones and rendered the figure of a primordial goddess for modern taste by reviving forgotten lapidary techniques.

The Owls and the Microcosm Collections both draw on the world of Nature but each treats it in a different way. In the first Collection the owl is represented in diverse abstract forms in miniature scale; the potent symbolism embodied by the bird is respected in the handling of forms and the master craftsmen who fashioned these works emphasized the eyes, windows of wisdom, thus endowing each bird with a personality of its own. The insects, on the contrary, are rendered as naturalistically as possible, enlarged in order to enhance their delicacy and to stress the structure and function of the joints. In both collections Lalaounis used silver and colorful minerals.

Wild Flowers, one of his most impressive and admired collections, captivates the viewer with the goldsmith's attention to intricate detail. Intrigued by botany, Lalaounis created almost life-size works in gleaming gold, set upon semiprecious stones. In the year 2000, Lalaounis returned to micro-sculptures, producing a series inspired by recent discoveries in Genetics and declaring his intention of creating collections of micro-sculptures rather than jewelry, from now on. These remarkable objects based on the molecular structure of DNA, make ample use of colorful stones and rise as slender monuments. In all his collections Lalaounis avoids excess, keeping to the size of table-top ornaments, combining inspiration and imagination to create *objets d'art* that are tangible manifestations of his axiom: "every creation has a story to tell".

The works for this exhibition have been chosen on merit and significance, as attuned to the values and objectives of the Onassis Cultural Center. We believe that the exhibition of selected *objets d'art* by Lalaounis, complemented by corresponding texts, is not only a notable contribution to the cultural activities organized by the Alexander S. Onassis Public Benefit Foundation but also an opportunity to give New Yorkers a vivid picture of this modern Greek goldsmith.

At this stage I would like to notably thank Mr. Stelio Papadimitriou, President of the Alexander S. Onassis Public Benefit Foundation (USA) for inviting the Ilias Lalaounis Jewelry Museum to mount this exhibition in its recently founded Cultural Center in New York. Our appreciation to all members of the Board of Trustees, and especially Mr. Paul Ioannidis for handling with such care all the preparatory organization.

I should also like to thank Ambassador Loucas Tsilas, Executive Director of the Foundation, for his support in this project and for facilitating the installation of the micro-sculptures in the exhibition space of the Onassis Cultural Center, and Ms. Amalia Cosmetatou for her assistance in every stage of this project.

A heartfelt thank you to all personnel, permanent and temporary, of the Ilias Lalaounis Jewelry Museum and Greek Gold S. A. for their help in organizing this exhibition and producing the accompanying catalogue; and above all to Ilias I. Lalaounis for entrusting me with the administration and recording of his creations, often nicknamed "his other children".

IOANNA LALAOUNIS-TSOUKOPOULOU

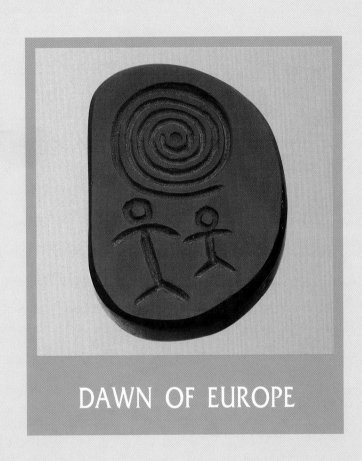

DAWN OF EUROPE

DAWN OF EUROPE COLLECTION, 1976

The Dawn of Europe Collection was inspired by the Old Stone Age and stimulated by the ideal of a united Europe. Lalaounis designed and presented it in 1976, as a tribute to the ideal of the European Union, particularly its political expression, as well as to the common prehistoric sources of modern artists. The collection comprises *objets d' art,* ornaments and figurines, whose prototypes are cave paintings and rock carvings.

The people inhabiting the Palaeolithic Dordogne and Altamira communicated through images. Lalaounis admits his fascination with these early images, which he sees as the earliest expressions of a common language. The cave paintings in France, Spain, Portugal and elsewhere, although in different geographical regions display common traits yet an autonomous and homogeneous development. Lalaounis perceived that the similarities in our respective languages far outnumber the differences imposed by time and culture. Furthermore, he discerned in these images a common source of inspiration for many twentieth-century artists who sought abstraction in 'primitive' art. For him these abstract images mean the essence of communication, which is, in his view, but one step away from the written word.

The collection comprises images from the prehistoric world transferred to micro-sculptures in semiprecious stones, rock-crystal and obsidian gems and silver imprints. The representations fall into three main thematic groups: anthropomorphic figures, zoomorphic figures and abstract designs with an emphasis on linear drawing, pictorial and peculiar symbolism. Scenes of hunting and of combat, ceremonial dances, masks and mother goddesses, taken from cave paintings at Valltorta in eastern Spain and rock-carvings at Tourves in France, are rendered on intaglio gems.

Parietal art and stone sculpture are the aesthetic manifestations of major human achievements: adjustment to the natural environment, principles of social organization, development of hunting techniques, even the emergence of religious sentiments. The female deity represented in a schist idol from Monte do Outeiro (Aljustel) in Portugal, inspired Lalaounis's designs on rock crystal 'moulds' from which silver 925° casts were made, while the religious art of Haut-Alentejo and Montemor-o-Novo in Portugal inspired two other works representing the "Magus".

The figurines or idols are independent works, free-standing or set on a base. The intaglios are flat and exhibited laid on a showcase stand. The cutting of the gem and the manipulation of its color allude to the original works in two ways: the rough outline of the gem recalls the surface of the cave walls on which prehistoric man painted, while its monochromy contrives to compound this effect: murky-white rock crystal and black obsidian for the matrix and dull gray for the silver stamp bring to mind the gloomy interior of caverns.

The contradistinction of ancient and modern is affected by other sources of inspiration and creation. When this collection was conceived, black-and-white photography had been ousted in favor of color, and relegated to use for the outdated, the timeworn, the primitive, as Lalaounis saw it. So it is not accidental that rock crystal, obsidian and silver were the materials selected for the works in this collection. They project a certain mystical quality, attractive for its antique connotations as well as for its modern look. Positive and negative, new versus old; the gemstones are the modern artist's canvas, as the cave walls were the prehistoric masters'.

As Lalaounis has said, so-called primitive art has often stimulated him to expression through his craft. "…*I feel like an apprentice each time I examine the works created by the old masters of prehistory or by unknown folk artists around the globe. I try to understand their various techniques, which are sometimes of astounding perfection. Above all, however, I strive to capture the spirit in which they were conceived. I believe that recourse to the source of art helps the artist to understand himself better - all the more so, since I believe that all works of art have some roots in the distant past. Every artist carries within him, consciously or unconsciously, the entire artistic heritage bequeathed to us by the past. I am neither an archaeologist nor an ethnologist. I have not, therefore, ventured into establishing this or that chronological sequence or geograph-*

ical pattern, intended to classify these works according to their age or their origins. I have rather attempted to see so-called primitive art as a whole. As such it spans the millennia, from the Paleolithic Age to the present day, and extends over all latitudes and longitudes of the globe. In fact no society exists that has not produced its own specific art, thus confirming that art lies deep in the foundations of man's existence.

In studying this vast field I have endeavored to identify the essential elements of primitive art, to understand its evolution and, above all, to comprehend its deeper meaning.

In my opinion, the moment man began to discover the component elements of form, began to analyze the structure of things in his subconscious mind, is a unique one in the history of mankind."

All the creations in the Dawn of Europe Collection are original in their design, materials and techniques as well as their modern appearance. Three basic aspects of man's existence - procuring food, conflict and religion -are repeated throughout as motifs epitomizing cave culture. The Dawn of Europe Collection demonstrates that contemporary Europe's aspiration to speak "with one voice" goes back thousands of years. Here Lalaounis stresses the ecumenical character of art and in particular the imperceptible divide between abstract images and writing, as an analogy for emphasizing the similarities rather than the differences imposed by time upon the languages and cultures of the Old Continent. The Dawn of Europe Collection is Ilias Lalaounis's contribution to transforming a vision into reality.

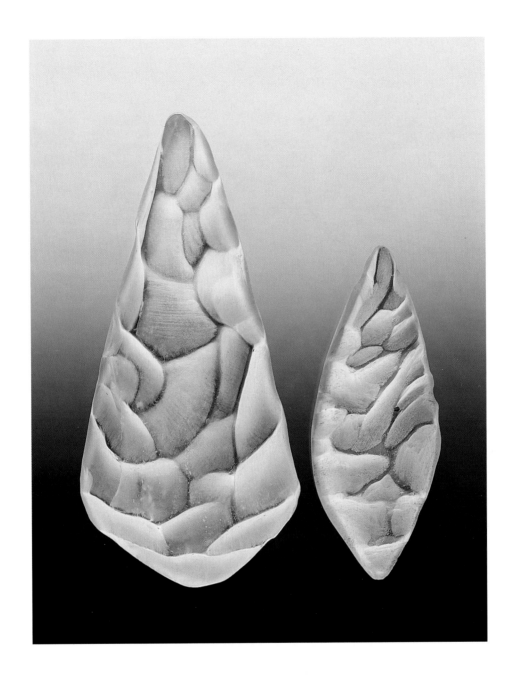

1. Two obelisks inspired from a paleolithic tool.
These modern works reconstruct a laurel-shaped blade
which was found in Solutre of France and date from 20.000 BC.

Rock crystal, JM 989554/95 and JM 989556/95

2. *Objet d'art* shaped as an obelisk and inspired
by an ovoid pendant found in Lalinde in the Dordogne, France
and dating from *c.* 8.000 BC.

Rock crystal with sodalite base, JM 989542/95

3. Intaglio inspired by an anthropomorphic motif found at
Estrecho de Santange, in Almeria of Spain,
dating from the 3rd millennium BC.
The stylized figure is depicted with raised hands.

Silver, JM 989501/95
Obsidian, JM 9888501/95

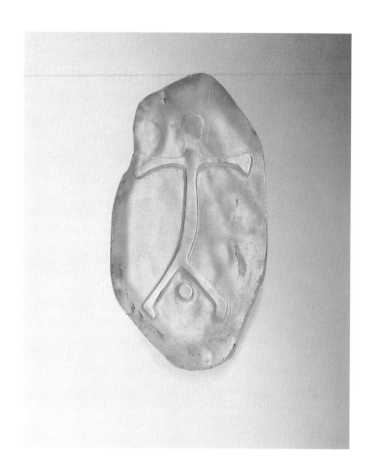

4. Intaglio inspired by cruciform anthropomorphic
figures from Roc de les Creus de Conet in France,
dating from the 3rd millennium BC.

Rock crystal, JM 989502/95

5. Intaglio inspired by a rock painting
discovered in Tagos valley, in Portugal,
dating from the second half of the 3rd millennium BC.
A scene of two figures standing under a spiral
symbolizing the sun.

Obsidian, JM 989503/95

6. Intaglio of an archer inspired by a rock painting
from Cueva de la Vieja, in Spain,
dating from 6500-5500 BC.

Silver, JM 989504/95
Rock crystal, JM 989504/95

7. Intaglio inspired by a fish depicted on a Minoan
vase from the palace of Phaistos in Crete, dating from
the Middle Minoan II period (2000-1700 BC).

Rock crystal, JM 989523/95

8. Intaglio with human figures,
equipped with tools and daggers,
inspired by a rock carving
found in the Val des Merveilles, France, and dating
from the first half of the 2nd millennium BC.

Rock crystal, JM 989541/95

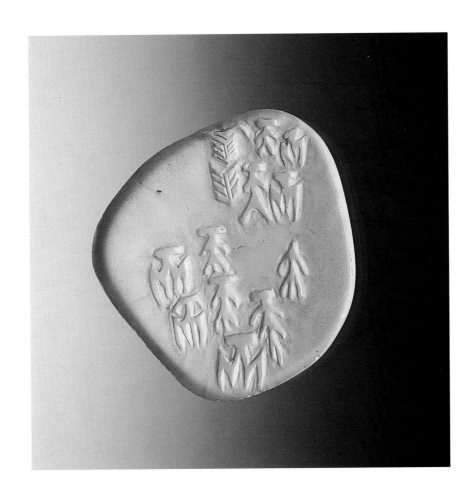

9. Intaglio with pairs of human figures,
male and female, inspired by a rock painting
found at Fuencaliente, Spain, and dating from the
second half of the 3rd millennium BC.

Rock crystal, JM 989546/95

10. A bas-relief depicting a woman holding a bison's horn.
This modern creation is inspired by the Late Stone Age
relief of the Laussel Venus, dating from 20.000 B.C.

Rock crystal, JM 989551/95

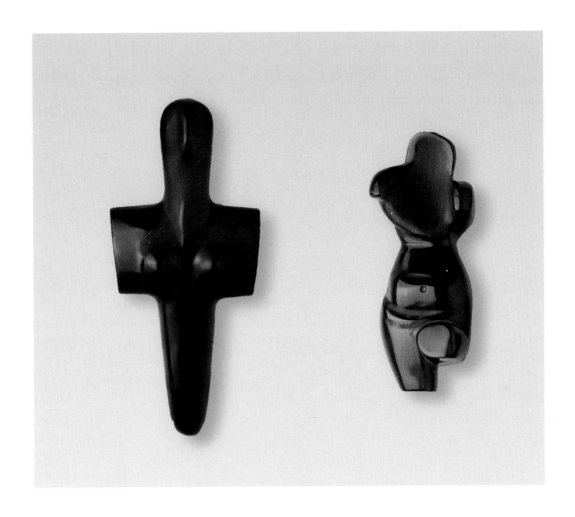

11. a. *Objet d'art* inspired by a Neolithic cruciform figurine
found at Senorbi, Sardinia (left).

Obsidian, JM 989608/95

b. *Objet d'art* in the form of a female torso, inspired by a type of
Neolithic figurine found in many parts of Europe (right).

Obsidian, JM 989609/95

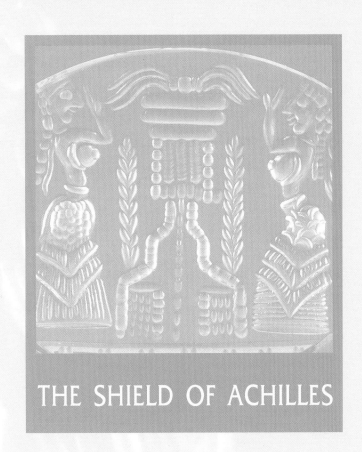

THE SHIELD OF ACHILLES

THE SHIELD OF ACHILLES COLLECTION, 1978

In the "Shield of Achilles" Collection, Lalaounis manifests his fascination with Aegean Bronze Age glyptics and his adoration for ancient Greek literature. To achieve this he set two tasks: he selected designs from thousands of intaglio seal-stones, especially the bezels of finger rings. He then employed these to represent the scenes described in Rhapsody XVIII of Homer's *Iliad*. Verses 468 to 608 narrate how Hephaistos, the divine metal-smith, was commissioned to fashion a new shield for Achilles (the Achaean hero fighting at Troy), hence the title of the Collection. Lalaounis illustrates Homer's world using forms and figures drawn from Minoan and Mycenean art, which is in a way contemporary to the events the poet recounts.

In his description of Achilles' shield, Homer conjures up a mental picture of mortal life in peace and war – activities in the ancient city, bucolic and agricultural occupations, pursuits such as hunting. Homer's poems hark back to an earlier Heroic Age, spanning the Early Mycenaean to the Geometric period and incorporating material from different eras.

Lalaounis created over 200 rock-crystal gems, of which 89 are presented in this Exhibition. Their intaglio devices derive from their counterparts in Bronze Age seal-carving, covering a wide repertoire of subjects –deities, humans, animals, abstract images or scenes. Lalaounis felt that the revival of the craft of glyptics was long overdue, and in creating the Shield of Achilles Collection he took the initiative of inspiring "the return to the art of Fabergé", that of gem cutting.

The representations on Lalaounis's gems fall into twelve thematic units, corresponding to his division of the contents of Rhapsody XVIII. They are exquisitely engraved on the tiny surfaces of rock crystal, oval (3.6 x 2.7 cm) or circular (approx. diam. 3 cm) and barely 0.5 cm thick, executed in intricate detail and filling the entire field so that the beholder can recognize them easily with the naked eye. These modern intaglios succeed in rendering, in whole or in part, the representations of ancient seal-stones, through the prism of Lalaounis's personal visual perception of Homer's vivid poetic descriptions.

Inspired by verses 468 onwards, the Collection begins with a representation of the *cosmos* (thematic unit one). Lalaounis chose a figure-of-eight shield, an allusion to the shape of the Creto-Mycenaean shield, and continued with imprints of the earth, the heavens, the sea and the "unwearied sun"…His thematic unit two relies on Homer's description of a city where there is a feasting in the streets and a wedding illustrated by women dancing. In thematic unit three he shows the brawl that takes place later, in the market place, with the assembled Elders arbitrating and judging.

Thematic units four, five and six show another city under siege, preparations afoot to ambush the foe's flocks and herds, and to attack the enemy army. The modern seal-stones show armor, weaponry, flocks of livestock, chariots, human figures in combat or hunting.

In thematic unit seven, which focuses on rustic tasks, the motifs of bunches of grapes and ears of wheat, the sacrifice of a bull and other related scenes are inspired by Minoan seal-stones. By way of contrast, in thematic units eight and nine, the lively depiction of a lion attacking a bull is a subject to which much attention is paid in works contemporary with the Epic. The seal engravings focus on the suppleness of the animal bodies as well as the ferocity and viciousness of beasts in combat.

To counteract the tension in these units, Lalaounis, in the last three units, conveys the gradual de-escalation of Homer's Rhapsody, as it comes to an end. Thematic unit ten shows animals grazing and suckling; unit eleven a dance in a city resembling Knossos, with gems representing its architectural structures, dancers and acrobats, and a lyre capturing the festive spirit. The final unit is a pictorial impression of Homer's words "the great might of the river Oceanus", including stylized waves, fish, ships and abstract motifs symbolizing the perpetuity of the watery element.

The gems in the Shield of Achilles Collection enhance both the genre idiom of the Homeric text and the essential humanism of Aegean Bronze Age art. In this modern revival of an ancient craft, Lalaounis pays homage to ancient art. But surely his most significant contribution is the creation of a series of interrelated gems that are not just independent works but integral parts of the narrative of the ancient Epic.

(THEMATIC UNIT 1) verses 468-489: [Hephaestus] «… went unto his bellows, and he turned these towards the fire and bade them work. And the bellows, twenty in all, blew upon the melting-vats, sending forth a ready blast of every force, now to further him as he laboured hard, and again in whatsoever way Hephaestus might wish and his work go on. And on the fire he put stubborn bronze and tin and precious gold and silver; and thereafter he set on the anvil-block a great anvil, and took in one hand a massive hammer, and in the other took the tongs. First fashioned he a shield, great and sturdy, adorning it cunningly in every part, and round about it set a bright rim, threefold and glittering, and therefrom made fast a silver baldric. Five were the layers of the shield itself, and on it he wrought many curious devices with cunning skill.

Therein he wrought the earth, therein the heavens, therein the sea, and the unwearied sun, and the moon at the full, and therein all the constellations wherewith heaven is crowned – the Pleiades, and the Hyades and the mighty Orion, and the Bear, that men call also the Wain, that circleth ever in her place and watcheth Orion, and alone hath no part in the baths of Ocean.»

(THEMATIC UNIT 2) verses 490-496 «Therein fashioned he also two cities of mortal men exceeding fair. In the one there were marriages and feastings, and by the light of the blazing torches they were leading the brides from their bowers through the city, and loud rose the bridal song. And young men were whirling in the dance, and in their midst flutes and lyres sounded continually; and there the women stood each before her door and marvelled.»

(THEMATIC UNIT 3) verses 497-508: «But the folk were gathered in the place of assembly; for there a strife had arisen, and two men were striving about the blood-price of a man slain; the one avowed that he had paid all, declaring his cause to the people, but the other refused to accept aught; and each was fain to win the issue on the word of a daysman. Moreover, the folk were cheering both, showing favour to this side and that. And the heralds held back the folk, and the elders were sitting upon polished stones in the sacred circle, holding in their hand the staves of the loud-voiced heralds. Therewith then would they spring up and give judgment, each in turn. And in the midst lay two talents of gold, to be given to him whoso among them should utter the most righteous judgment.»

(THEMATIC UNIT 4) verses 509-519: «But around the other city lay in leaguer two hosts of warriors gleaming in armour. And twofold plans found favour with them, either to lay waste the town or to divide in portions twain all the substance that the lovely city contained within. Howbeit the besieged would nowise hearken thereto, but were arming to meet the foe in ambush. The wall were their dear wives and little children guarding, as they stood thereon, and therewithal the men that were holden of old age; but the rest were faring forth, led of Ares and Pallas Athene.»

(THEMATIC UNIT 5) verses 520-529: «But when they were come to the place where it seemed good unto them to set their ambush, in a river-bed where was a watering-place for all herds alike, there they sate them down, clothed about with flaming bronze. Thereafter were two scouts set by them apart from the host, waiting till they should have sight of the sheep and sleek cattle. And these came presently, and the two herdsmen followed with them playing upon pipes; and of the guile wist they not at all. But the liers-in-wait, when they saw these coming on, rushed forth against them and speedily cut off the herds of cattle and fair flocks of white-fleeced sheep, and slew the herdsmen withal.»

(THEMATIC UNIT 6) verses 530-540: «But the besiegers, as they sat before the places of gathering and heard much tumult among the kine, mounted forthwith behind their high-stepping horses, and set out thitherward, and speedily came upon them. Then set they their battle in array and fought beside the river banks, and were ever smiting one another without a wound, and another she dragged dead through the mellay by the feet; and the raiment that she had about her shoulders was red with the blood of men. Even as living mortals joined they in the fray and fought; and they were hauling away each the bodies of the others' slain.»

(THEMATIC UNIT 7) verses 541-575: «therein he set also soft fallow-land, rich tilth and wide, that was three times ploughed; and ploughers full many therein were wheeling their yokes and driving them this way and that. And whensoever after turning they came to the headland of the field, then would a man come forth to each and give into his hands a cup of honey-sweet wine; and the ploughmen would turn them in the furrow, eager to reach the headland of the deep tilth. And the field grew black behind and seemed verily as it had been ploughed, for all that it was of fold; herein was the great marvel of the work.

Therein he set also a king's demesne-land, wherein labourers were reaping, bearing sharp sickles in their hands. Some handfuls were falling in rows to the ground along the swathe, while others, the binders of sheaves, were binding with twisted ropes of straw. Three binders stood hard by them, while behind them boys would gather the handfuls, and bearing them in their arms would busily give them to the binders; and among them the king, staff in hand, was standing in silence at the swath, joying in his heart. And heralds apart beneath an oak were making ready a feast, and were dressing a great ox they had slain for sacrifice; and the women sprinkled the flesh with white barley in abundance, for the worker's mid-day meal.

Therein he set a vineyard heavily laden with clusters, a vineyard fair and wrought of gold; black were the grapes and the vines were set up throughout on silver poles, . . . and one single path led thereto, whereby the vintagers went and came, whensoever they gathered the vintage. And maidens and youths in childish glee were bearing the honey-sweet fruit in wicker baskets. And in their midst a boy made pleasant music with a clear-toned lyre and thereto sang sweetly the Linos-song with his delicate voice; and his fellows beating the earth in unison therewith followed on with bounding feet mid dance and shoutings.»

(THEMATIC UNIT 8) verses 576-583: «And therein he wrought a herd of straight-horned kine. And with lowing hasted they forth from the byre to pasture beside the sounding river, beside the waving reed. And golden were the herdsmen that walked beside the kine, four in number, and nine dogs swift of foot followed after them. But two dread lions amid the foremost kind were holding a loud-lowing bull, and he, bellowing mightily was haled of them, while after him pursued the dogs and young men. The lions twin had rent the hide of the great bull, and were devouring the inward parts and the black blood, …»

(THEMATIC UNIT 9) verses 583-586: «...while the herdsmen vainly sought to fright them, tarring on the swift hound. Howbeit these shrank from fastening on the lions, but stood hard by and barked and sprang aside.»

(THEMATIC UNIT 10) verses 587-589: «Therein also the famed god of the two strong arms wrought a pasture in a fair dell, a great pasture of white-fleeced sheep, and folds, and roofed huts, and pens.»

(THEMATIC UNIT 11) verses 590-606: «Therein furthermore the famed god of the two strong arms cunningly wrought a dancing-floor like unto that which in wide Cnosus Daedalus fashioned of old for fair-tressed Ariadne. There were many youths dancing and maidens of the price of many cattle, holding their hands upon the wrists one of the other. Of these the maidens were clad in fine linen, while the youths wore well-woven tunics faintly glistering with oil; and the maidens had fair chaplets, and the youths had daggers of gold hanging from silver baldrics. Now would they run round with cunning feet exceedingly lightly; and now again would they run in rows towards each other. And a great company stood around the lovely dance, taking joy therein; and two tumblers whirled up and down through the midst of them as leaders in the dance.»

(THEMATIC UNIT 12) verses 607-608: «Therein he set also the great might of the river Oceanus, around the uttermost rim of the strongly-wrought shield.»

*(from the English translation by A.T. Murray for the Loeb Classical Library).

OWLS

OWLS COLLECTION, 1975

The owl as a symbol and an attribute in Antiquity inspired Lalaounis to create his Owls and Anthemia Collection. First presented in 1975, it epitomizes his idea of creating *objets d' art* that vivify the spirit of Classical Hellas. His conviction that he would succeed in this endeavor was based not only on his intuitive interest in archaeology, but also on his firm belief that ancient forms are an inspiration for creating modern works of art.

The owl is inextricably associated with Athens, capital *par excellence* of Classical Greek civilization, and with its patron goddess, Athena, personification of wisdom and victory. Further elaboration of the owl's form led to its correlation and identification with the inverted *anthemion* (palmette) and the Ionic column, two other typical motifs of Classical civilization. Here we present one part of this Collection, the micro-sculptures in the form of owls.

In these modern micro-sculptures, Lalaounis was concerned not so much with reproducing the form of the owl as with rendering its characteristics so that it was immediately recognizable to all. Bearing in mind the principles of artistic expression and the objective of creating a unified collection, he opted for the standing owl as his main subject. He then proceeded to model its body in ovoid and spherical forms, no more than 25 cm high, in dimensions appropriate to table-top ornaments. The head was fashioned as a sphere or an ellipsoid, with prominent eyes, in some instances exaggerated to the point of substituting for it. The form of each owl can be broken down clearly into simple geometric structures. In other words, the result of the artistic elaboration was not a naturalistic representation of the bird, but a synthesis that symbolizes its substance.

Lalaounis worked on hundreds of designs, with enthusiasm and sophistication. He commonly makes multiple designs before selecting a few to embody his idea. This tactic enables him to proceed to his general strategy of choosing appropriate materials and creating a series of independent works that harmoniously compose a balanced collection of three-dimensional micro-sculptures. The designs, moreover, enabled the artist to familiarize himself with the owl's morphological features, its poses and movements.

Silver and gold were handled with inordinate skill to produce about 150 works, while semi-precious stones were used to convey the iridescent plumage. Here the stones were intended to emphasize the symbolic, non-naturalistic character of the creations —rose quartz, sodalite, obsidian, aventurine, rock crystal, amethyst and so on— all consistent with the personal style and tradition of Lalaounis's workshop, all with strong hues that accentuate the anatomical features of the owls.

When describing the process of giving his designs concrete form, Lalaounis always gives great credit to his craftsmen. In this Collection in particular, he recalls how the owls came alive in the hands of the masters, as they modelled these birds, each with its own expressive qualities, as if each had a personality of its own. The craftsmen emphasized the eyes and named each piece according to the emotions its facial features evoked. So the viewer can search for the "curious owl", the "wise owl", the "dubious owl" and so on, appellations that they retain to this day, giving each a distinct identity.

This Collection, with its admirable combination of traditional concepts, modern forms, experience in handling materials and applying techniques, is emblematic of Lalaounis's career. The horizons of his creative spirit continue to expand, with the further elaboration and understanding of the plasticity of forms in objects, endowed with a personal style for a universal taste.

1. Design for an owl micro-sculpture.

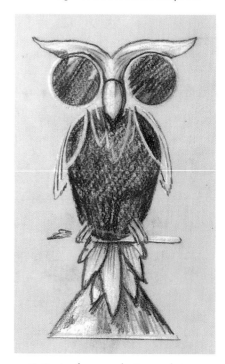

2. Design for an owl micro-sculpture.

3. "THE MATHEMATICAL OWL".
An apellation referring to
its geometrically shaped head.

Silver and sodalite on a rose quartz base.

JM 895101/01

4. "IF ONLY I WERE A BUTTERFLY..."

Rose quartz and silver on a rose quartz base.

LL881491

5. "THE CURIOUS OWL".

Silver and obsidian on an amazonite base.

JM 881481/01

6. Design for an owl micro-sculpture.

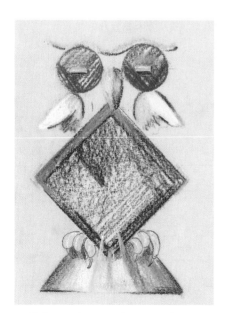

7. Design for an owl micro-sculpture.

8. "GETTING MORE AND MORE CURIOUS".

Four owls forming a branch in silver, with sodalite
eyes, on an amethyst base.

JM 881561/01

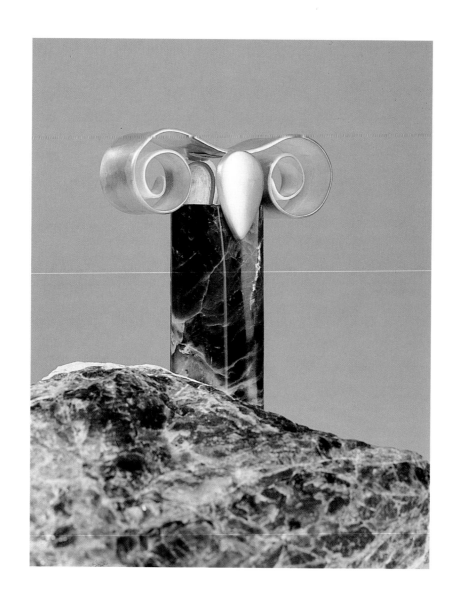

9. "THE IONIC OWL".
Mimicry develops from living too long
among ancient Ionic columns.

Sodalite and silver on a sodalite base.

JM 881551/01

10. A wise little owlet in rock crystal
embellished with silver on a
solid rock crystal base.

JM 881461/01

11. "THE ALERT OWL".
The wide-open eyes and the textured
surface of this owl's body, portray the bird of prey.

Silver.

JM S16/70/95

12. Dark but not ominous, this bird seems to
glow with an inner light.

Obsidian.

LL 895091

13. Design for an owl micro-sculpture.

14. Design for an owl micro-sculpture.

15. Design for a pendant.

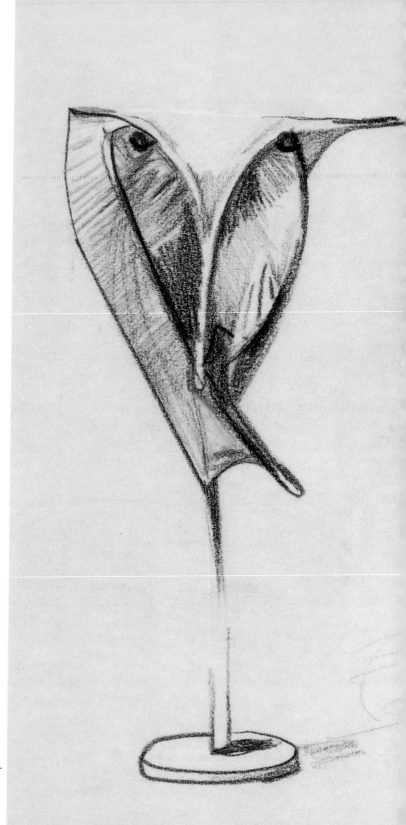

16. "THE HEART-SHAPED OWL".
*"Kinetic art is a product of the wisdom and imagination of the sculptors of our age;
we have used this form of artistic expression in creating this owl".* I.L.

Silver on an amazonite base.

JM 881581/01

WILD FLOWERS

WILD FLOWERS COLLECTION, 1970

Ilias Lalaounis's love of botany has led him to create many collections inspired by the natural environment. "Wild Flowers" is a collection of *objets d' art* inspired by the flora of the Greek and the Mediterranean landscape. Its stimulus can be traced to Nike A. Goulandris's publication *Wild Flowers of Greece*, which presents the wonderful world of the plants that grow in the Greek countryside. Over 100 of the illustrated specimens indigenous to Greece provided Lalaounis with the initial data for creating this collection.

As he himself declared, his ambition was to recreate allegorically the plant forms and to demonstrate the technical skills of the master goldsmiths in his workshop. The final result demanded assiduous attention to detail, and the painstaking preparation of the flowers took many months. Lalaounis and his assistants had first to grasp the essentials –the actual dimensions of the plants and their natural habitats–, then to choose the appropriate materials and last to proceed to the elaboration of the pieces. To achieve accuracy in rendering the forms involved careful study of the frailty of the stems, the sharpness of the thorns, the velvety texture of the petals.

As a diligent student of ancient techniques, Lalaounis guided his craftsmen to use gold and silver as the only materials suitable for reproducing the delicate floral forms, and semi-precious stones to evoke the rocks and ground of their natural habitat. The ductility of gold enabled the goldsmith to achieve elegance of line, while its malleability permitted him to apply such complicated yet effective techniques as repoussé, filigree and intricate work in gold leaf. The richness of the material and the wealth of minutiae in these *objets d' art* create a luxurious impression. The leaves, the branches, the stalks and the petals are all presented in intimate detail, endowing the pieces with an incredible quality of naturalism. The deep hues of the semi-precious stones correspond sensitively to the real colors of the crags and ravines of the Greek mountains.

These exquisite creations of Nature need no stylization, no transformation, no interpretation; all they ask is respect for their living form, their size, their weight and a balance in keeping with their surroundings.

1. THISTLE
Carlina utzka

Silver, gold-plated,
presented on a
sodalite base.

JM 880901/95

2. BELLFLOWER
Campanula foliosa

Silver, gold-plated,
presented on an
amethyst base.

JM 880902/95

3. AARON'S ROD
Euphorbia characias

Silver, gold-plated,
presented on a
sodalite base.

JM 880903/95

4. PEONY
Paeonia peregrina

Silver, gold-plated, presented on a amethyst base.

JM 880908/95

5. ORCHID
Orchis simia

Silver, gold-plated,
presented on a
mineral base.

JM 880911/95

6. HOUSE-LEEK
Sempervivum reginae amaliae

Silver, gold-plated, presented on a rose quartz base.

JM 880912/95

7. WILD ROSE
Rosa canina

Silver, gold-plated,
presented on an
amethyst base.

JM 880914/95

8. DANDELION
Taraxacum officinale

Silver, gold-plated, presented on a mineral base.

JM 880916/95

9. POPPY
Anemone panovina

Silver, gold-plated,
presented on an
aventurine base.

JM 880904/95

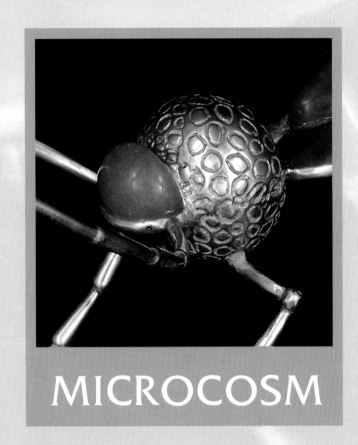

MICROCOSM

MICROCOSM COLLECTION, 1974

In this collection the artist turned to one of Nature's most remarkable phenomena: the microcosm of insects, which pre-dates man's existence by millions of years and seems destined to outlive the human race. Ilias Lalaounis wondered at the ideal physical and organic qualities of insects, their refined and complicated structure. He admired the smooth suppleness of the caterpillar, the elegance of the wasp's waist, the apparently fragile yet incredibly strong legs of the grasshopper. He was also inspired by popular traditions about insects: the ever-busy worker bee, the good-for-nothing drone, the carefree cicada and the provident ant.

The enlargement of natural forms is a distinctive and recurrent characteristic in Lalaounis's *oeuvre*. This is his way of emphasizing the attributes of an organism, thus enabling the beholder to appreciate a life form that is oft misunderstood.

Lalaounis used silver to construct the main body of his insects and semi-precious stones to enhance features such as their eyes or other anatomical details. The forms of these dignified, bold, crawling and buzzing arthropods inspired Lalaounis to create over 40 enlarged insect designs. Some are cute or creepy, others are symbolic of industry and dedication. Insects and spiders may not be everyone's favorite creatures, nevertheless they are necessary allies of mankind, for they pollinate countless crops and clean up the earth's surface by feeding on decaying matter. The ant has been fashioned standing and facing the viewer in playful pose; the hard-working bee is bent intent over her honeycomb; the spider climbs nimbly towards her web; the beetle ambles slowly protected by its shell; the grasshopper's alacrity is obvious from its flexible spindly legs.

Insects have been represented in art at least since the Middle Kingdom in Egypt. In Greek culture they appear in myths and folklore, frequently assuming the role of potent symbols or engaging metaphors. The religious or symbolic connotations of insects have remained the same over the centuries and in different cultures, depending on their position in the food chain and their special function. It is no accident that Lalaounis has designed dozens of butterflies; their metamorphosis (the title of his first publication) is at once a sign of good luck and a symbol of rebirth.

Lalaounis was also influenced by the fact that insects were studied by devotees of the Enlightenment in the eighteenth century and were, for a long time, a popular treasure beautifully displayed in private homes. Thus he proposes the Microcosm works as table-top ornaments rather than personal adornments, which were fashioned in the eighteenth and nineteenth centuries, culminating in the jewelry creations of the Art Nouveau period.

Lalaounis once again admired Nature's ingenuity and simulated it in an original and arresting manner. His enlarged insects can be observed and enjoyed, displayed against the earthy warmth of semi-precious stones.

1. ANT

Silver, sodalite, rock
crystal and garnet.

JM 881001/95

2. MIDGE

Silver, obsidian, rock
crystal and mica.

JM881011/95

3. ARTHROPOD

Silver and aventurine.

JM 881021/95

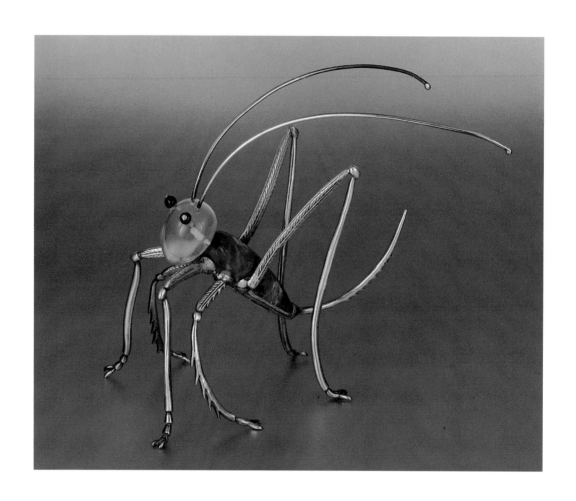

4. GRASSHOPPER

Silver, sodalite, rock crystal and garnet.

JM 881031/95

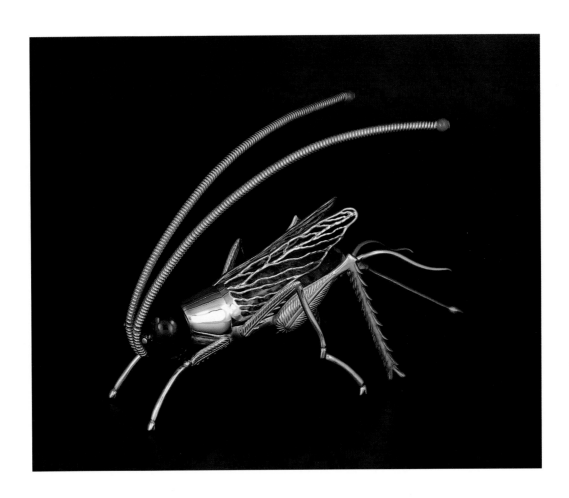

5. CICADA

Silver, sodalite, obsidian,
garnet and mica.

JM 881081/95

6. FLY

Silver, rodochrosite, rock
crystal, obsidian and mica.

JM 881131/95

7. BEE

Silver, sodalite and mica.

JM 881141/95

8. TURTLE

Silver.

JM881191/95

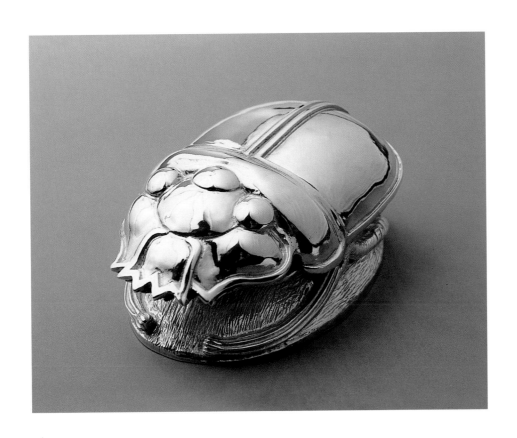

9. SCARAB

Silver.

JM881181/95

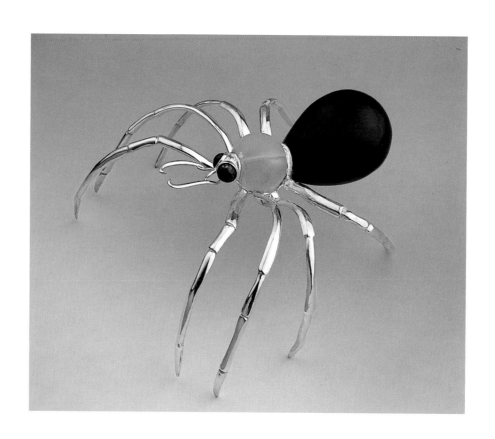

10. SPIDER

Silver, sodalite, obsidian
and rock crystal.

JM 881251/95

11. BUTTERFLY
Silver.
JM881121/95

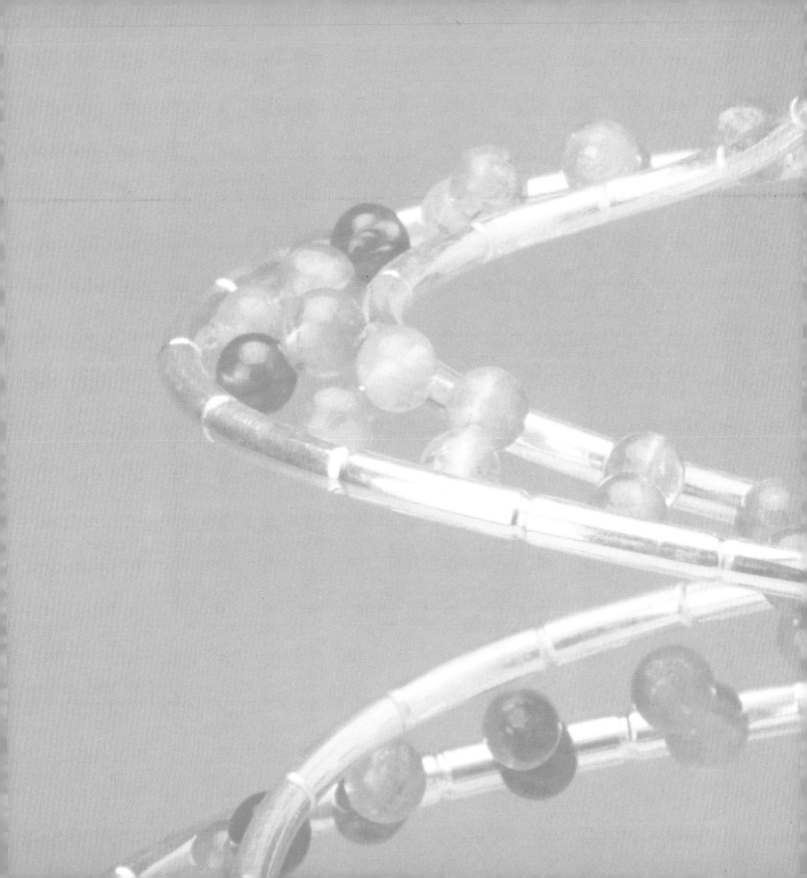

DNA

DNA COLLECTION, 2000

I lias Lalaounis is fascinated by the challenge of creating works of art from ideas. The DNA Collection is a splendid example of this transformation. His interest in recent developments in the field of genetics inspired him to design and produce micro-sculptures that transmute a fact of life into a *fait d' art*.

Avant-garde creations have often been associated with subjects invisible to the naked eye. The current discoveries in genetics, the study of the microcosm of the cell and the mapping of the genetic code, are helping to elucidate the evolution of mankind. Lalaounis effectively manipulates these biological data to render art forms, presenting the essence of life as an aesthetic statement. This singular naturalism is distinctive of Lalaounis's style.

He brings forth hundreds of designs for pieces that could be presented suspended in space. As parts of a single collection, the designs define objects of comparable dimensions. He specifies that these are to be of accessible size, that of table-top ornaments. He keeps them slender and elaborates their form using semi-precious stones, silver and gold to represent the genetic elements. What makes these designs appealing to the wider public is the fact that their structural components, based on human DNA codes, are easily recognized by the layman. Although

Lalaounis researched information in scientific papers and books intended for the specialist, this has been analyzed and reproduced as artistic motifs to suit the taste of his contemporary audience.

When describing his creations for the DNA Collection, Lalaounis observes that, "*The latest discoveries in biology have enabled us to grasp fully the enormous significance of DNA for our health and survival. Still we cannot disregard the aesthetic delicacy of the DNA double helix with its slanting bonds. The twisting spiral movement gives an impression of upward flight, while the bonds between the two closely entwined helixes reflect stability. What greater challenge for the artist than to render this wondrous entity through his work? And to present it not only as a jewel but also as an object to decorate a living room or a desk and so become part of everyday life. These were the thoughts behind the creation of a series of objects and pieces of jewelry that express this determinant factor of our existence and that of the generations to come*".

These simple yet sophisticated designs combine science and aesthetics. The dynamic line of their curvaceous and expressive forms evokes the life force of Nature.

1. *Objet d'art* inspired by chromosomes in the stage of mitosis, cell division, as seen through the microscope.

Rock crystal and 18ct gold on a base of obsidian.

JM 845171/00

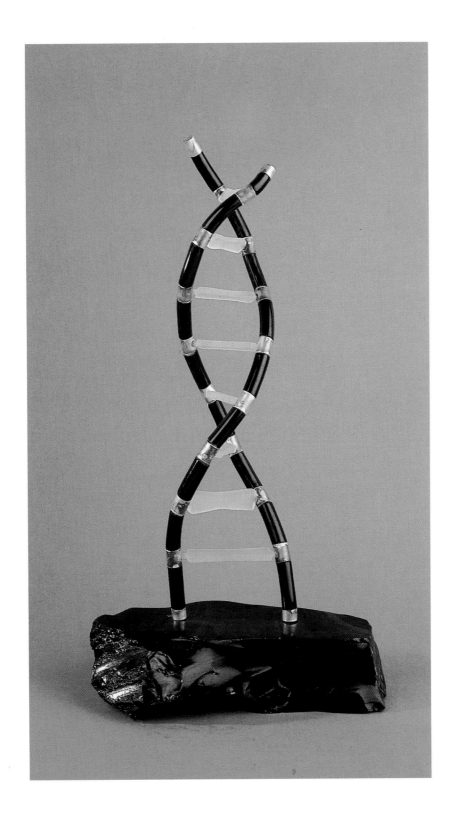

2. *Objet d'art* inspired by the double helix of DNA, as designed by biologists after studying the structure of DNA.

Rock crystal, obsidian and silver on a base of obsidian.

JM 845001/00

3. *Objet d'art* inspired by a helix
of nucleic acids forming DNA,
as this is shown in presentations
by geneticists.

Silver, tourmalines and semi-precious
stones on a base of amethyst.

JM 845061/00

4. *Objet d'art* inspired by RNA, a molecular assemblage forming the cycle of life, based on scientific presentations of this acid form.

Haematite and silver on a base of obsidian.

JM 845081/00

5. *Objet d'art* inspired by mitosis, the division of a cell into two "daughter" cells, as seen through the microscope.

Rock crystal, agate, plexiglass, and silver on a base of obsidian.

JM 845111/00

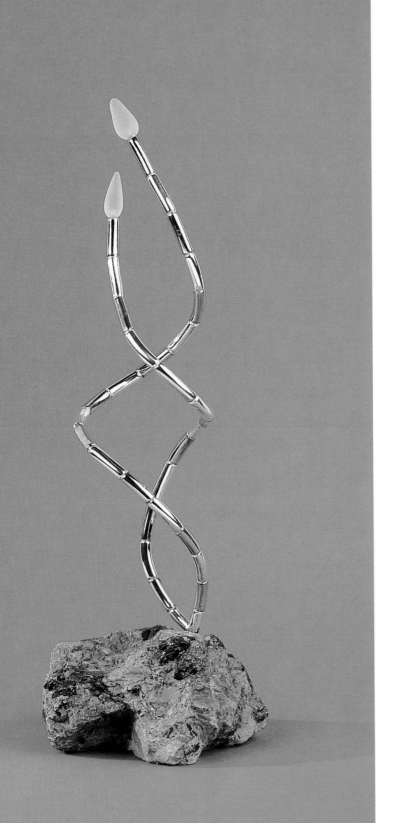

6. *Objet d'art* representing the DNA
double helix and its component parts.

Silver, copper and rock crystal
on a base of chalcosite.

JM 845005/00

7. *Objet d'art* inspired by the DNA helix, depicting the bonds between atoms of hydrogen, oxygen, carbon and phosphorus.

Rock crystal and semi-precious stones on a base of rock crystal.

JM 845021/00

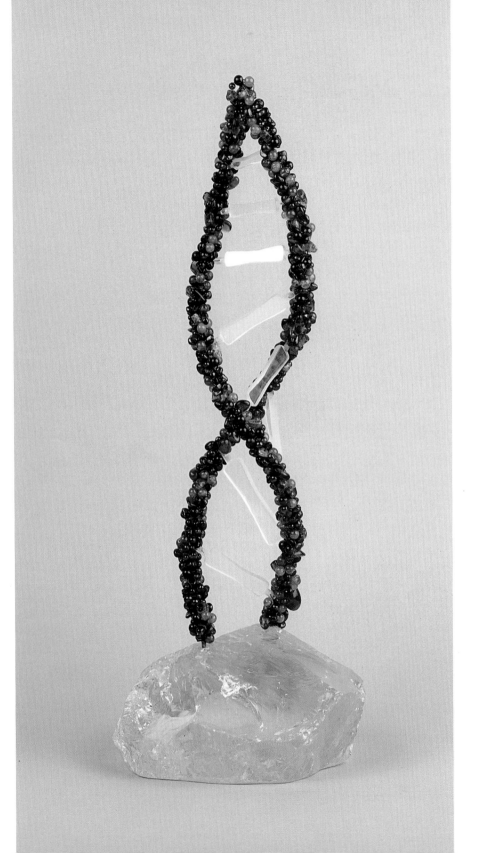

8. *Objet d'art* inspired by the DNA helix. The helix carries atoms of hydrogen, oxygen, carbon and phosphorus.

Rock crystal and semi-precious stones on a base of rock crystal.

JM 845011/00

9. *Objet d'art* inspired by an amylase spiral, as seen through the microscope.

Silver and semi-precious stones on a base of malachite.

JM 845151/00

10. Object inspired by atoms of phosphoric acid, as seen through the microscope. This is a dendriform *objet d'art*.

Gold and semi-precious stones on a base of rock crystal.

JM 845131/00

11. *Objet d'art* inspired by the DNA structure: A clasp which opens up, as seen through the microscope.

Silver and enamel on a base of obsidian.

JM 845051/00

12. *Objet d'art* inspired by the collagen triple helix, as presented by the geneticists.

Silver on a base of obsidian.

JM 845121/00

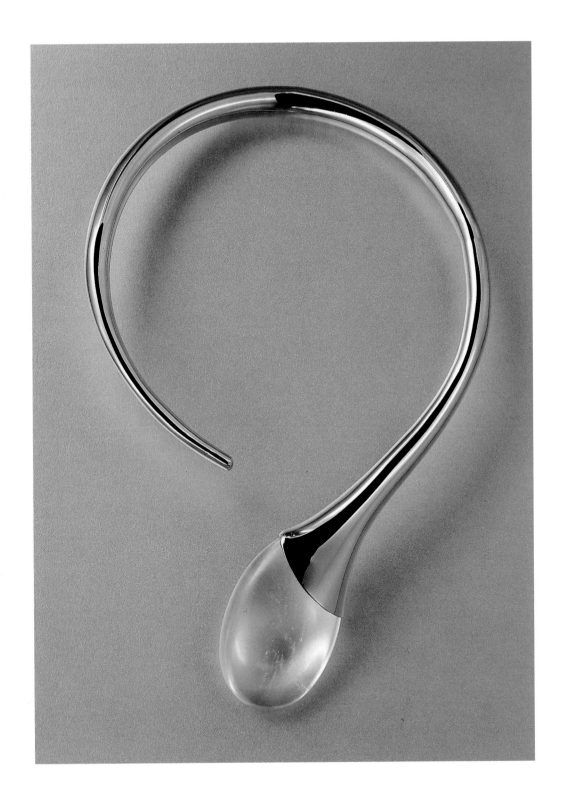

13. *Objet d'art* inspired by a spermatozoon, as seen through the microscope.

18 ct gold and rock crystal.

JM 845041/01

COLLECTIONS OF JEWELRY AND MICRO-SCULPTURES BY ILIAS LALAOUNIS

Minoan and Mycenean (1957)

Classical and Hellenistic (1957)

Swans and Dolphins (1957)

Bonnie and Clyde (1968)

Body Jewelry (1969)

Palaeolithic and Neolithic (1969, 1971)

Signs of the Zodiac (1970)

Byzantine (1970, 1976)

Wild Flowers of Greece (1970)

Biosymbols (1972)

Silver Frolics (1973)

Neogeometric (1973)

Motion in Space (1974)

Micrososm (1974)

Cycladic (1974)

Executive Boxes (1974)

Owls and Anthemia (1975)

Drops and Chitons (1975)

Dawn of Europe (1976)

From Luristan to Persepolis (1975)

Golf Players (1976)

Choreographism (1977)

Holy Land (1977, 1987)

Horseshoes (1977)

Chrysotektonemata (1977)

The Shield of Achilles (1978)

Seashells (1978)

Micro-sculpture from Minoan art (1979)

Katerini L. (1980)

Demetra L. (1981)

Far East (1981, 1982)

Ilion (1983, 1993)

Place Vendôme (1983)

For Every Woman's Victory (1984)

From the Walls of Constantinople to
the Tower of London: the Tudor
Collection (1985)

Mesopotamia (1986)

Arabesques (1988)

Süleyman the Magnificent (1988)

Islamic Art (1989)

Amerindian (1990)

Valentine (1990)

Nature and my Art (1990)

Pastorale (1990)

Cypriot (1991)

Celtic (1991)

Vikings (1991)

Scythian (1997)

DNA (2000)

CHAOS (2001)

SELECTED BIBLIOGRAPHY OF SOURCES CONSULTED BY THE ARTIST
DURING THE PRODUCTION OF HIS DESIGNS

Abélanet, Jean. *Signes sans paroles*. Paris, 1986.

Αλεξίου, Στυλιανός. *Μινωικός Πολιτισμός*. Ηράκλειο, 3η εκδ.(χ.χ.)

Bandi, Hans Georg et al. *L'Âge de Pierre*. Paris, 1960.

Bataille, Georges. *La peinture Préhistorique*. Genève, 1980.

Bazin, Germain. *A Gallery of Flowers*. London, 1960.

Berenguer, Magín. *Prehistoric Man and his Art*. London, 1973.

Boardman, John. *Greek Gems and Finger Rings. Early Bronze Age to Late Classical*.
    London, 1970.

Boardman, John. *Athenian Black Figure Vases*. London, 1974.

Boardman, John. *Athenian Red Figure Vases*. The Archaic Period. London, 1975.

Boardman, John. *Athenian Red Figure Vases*. The Classical Period. London, 1975.

Boardman, John et al. *L'art grec*. München and Paris, 1966.

Buchholz, Hans Georg - Karageorghis, Vassos. *Prehistoric Greece and Cyprus*.
    London, 1973.

Chadour-Sampson, Beatriz-Anna - Lalaounis-Tsoukopoulou, Ioanna (eds.).
    Modern Revival of Ancient Gold. Athens, 1998.

Charbonneaux, Jean - Martin, Roland - Villard, François. *Archaic Greek Art*. London,
    1971.

Giedion, Siegfried. *La naissance de l'art*. Bruxelles, 1965.

Goulandris, Nike. *Wild Flowers of Greece*. Athens, 1972.

Μουσείο Γουλανδρή (εκδ.). *Αγριολούλουδα της Ελληνικής Γης*. Αθήναι, 1965.

Head, S.N. - Σβορώνος, Νικόλαος. *Λεύκωμα Αρχαίων Ελληνικών Νομισμάτων*.
    Αθήναι, 1898

Higgins, Reynold. *Minoan and Mycenaean Art*. London, 19712.

Hood, Sinclair. *The Minoans. Crete in the Bronze Age*. London, 1971.

Lalaounis, Ilias (ed) *Metamorphoses*. Athens, 1984.

Λαλαούνης, Ηλίας. *Ευρωπαϊκή Χαραυγή*. Αθήνα, 1988.

Lalaounis, Ilias (ed.) *Wild Flowers of Greece. A Collection by Ilias Lalaounis*, Athens,
    1997.

Lane, Arthur. *Greek Pottery*. London, 1963.

Leroi-Gourhan, André. *Préhistoire de l'art occidental*. Paris, 1971.

Lommel, Andreas. *Προϊστορικός και Πρωτόγονος άνθρωπος*. Αθήνα, 1967.

Lullies, Reinhard. *Griechische Vasen der reifarchaischen Zeit*. München, 1953.

Marinatos, Spyridon. *Crete and Mycenae*. Athens, 1959.

Mylonas, Georgios E. *Mycenae and the Mycenaean Age*. Princeton, 1966.

Oakley, Kenneth P. *Man the Tool-Maker*. London, 1972.

Pfeifen, John. *The Cell*. New York, 1972.

Pini, Ingo. *Iraklion Archäologisches Museum*. Die Siegelabdrücke von Phästos, Corpus der Minoischen und Mykenischen Siegel, B. II Teil 5 (Matz, Friedrich - Pini, Ingo hrg.). Berlin, 1970.

Platon, Nikolaos. *Iraklion Archäologisches Museum*. Die Siegel der Vorpalastzeit, Corpus der Minoischen und Mykenischen Siegel, B. II Teil 1 (Matz, Friedrich - Pini, Ingo hrg.). Berlin, 1969.

Platon, Nikolaos - Pini, Ingo - Sallies, Gisela - Dessene, André. *Iraklion Archäologisches Museum. Die Siegel der Altpalastzeit*, Corpus der Minoischen und Mykenischen Siegel, B. II Teil 2 (Pini, Ingo hrg.). Berlin, 1977.

Robertson, Martin. *A History of Greek Art*. Cambridge, 1975.

Roussot, Alain. *Aspects de la Préhistoire en Aquitaine*. Bordeaux, 1978.

Sakellarakis, Jannis A. - Kenna, Victor E.G. *Iraklion Sammlung Metaxas*, Corpus der Minoischen und Mykenischen Siegel, B. IV (Matz, F. - Pini, I. hrg.). Berlin, 1969.

Sakellariou, Agnes. *Die Minoischen und Mykenischen Siegel des Nationalmuseums in Athen*, Corpus der Minoischen und Mykenishen Siegel, B. I (Matz, F. - Biesantz, H. hrg.). Berlin, 1964.

Sakellariou, Agnes - Papathanasopoulos, Georgios. *Musée Archéologique National. Collections Préhistoriques*. Athènes, 1965.

Sieveking, Ann. *The Cave Artists*. London, 1979.

Simon, Erika - Hirmer, Max & Albert. *Die griechischen Vasen*. München, 1976.

Sonneville-Bordes , Denise de. *La Préhistoire Moderne*. Perigueux 1972 .

Sparkes, Brian A. - Talcott, Lucy. *Pots and Pans of Classical Athens*. Princeton-New Jersey, 1976.

Θεοχάρης, Δημήτρης Ρ. *Νεολιθικός Πολιτισμός*. Αθήνα, 1981.

Thompson, Dorothy Burr. *The Athenian Agora. An Ancient Shopping Center*. Princeton-New Jersey, 1971.

Waechter, John. *Man before History*. Oxford, 1976.

Wegner, Max. *L' art grec*. Fribourg, n.d.

The Ilias Lalaounis Jewelry Museum in Athens was founded in 1993 and opened to the public as a non-profit institution in December 1994. Today the Museum houses in its permanent collections some 3000 models of jewelry and micro-sculptures from 50 collections designed by its founder Ilias Lalaounis between 1940 and 2000. The Museum also collects jewelry from different periods and various cultures. With an eye to the future, the Museum focuses on being an international center for the history of jewelry and the goldsmith's art. It organizes temporary exhibitions, research programs, publications and lectures. Further initiatives are social work and the educational programs for those with an interest in practical jewelry-making and design. The Ilias Lalaounis Jewelry Museum is the first museum for contemporary jewelry in Greece.

ILIAS LALAOUNIS JEWELRY MUSEUM
Karyatidon-Kallisperi Str.,
Acropolis, 117 42, Athens
Tel.: 9221044, Fax: 9237358
web site: www.lalaounis-jewelrymuseum.gr
e-mail: jewelrymuseum@ath.forthnet.gr